40
DAYS OF
DELIGHTING
IN GOD

MARY SWAIN

MarySwain

ISBN (paperback): 978-1-7395233-0-5
ISBN (eBook): 978-1-7395233-1-2

Unless otherwise identified, all scripture quotations are taken from THE HOLY BIBLE, NEW INTERNATIONAL VERSION®, NIV® Copyright © 1973, 1978, 1984, 2011 by Biblica, Inc.® Used by permission. All rights reserved worldwide.

Scripture quotations marked TPT are from The Passion Translation®. Copyright © 2017, 2018, 2020 by Passion & Fire Ministries, Inc. Used by permission. All rights reserved. ThePassionTranslation.com.

Scripture quotations marked AMP are taken from the Amplified® Bible (AMP), Copyright © 2015 by The Lockman Foundation. Used by permission. lockman.org

Scripture quotations marked NLT are taken from the Holy Bible, New Living Translation, copyright ©1996, 2004, 2015 by Tyndale House Foundation. Used by permission of Tyndale House Publishers, Carol Stream, Illinois 60188. All rights reserved.

Scripture quotations marked ESV are from The ESV® Bible (The Holy Bible, English Standard Version®), copyright © 2001 by Crossway, a publishing ministry of Good News Publishers. Used by permission. All rights reserved.

Scripture quotations marked KJV are taken from the King James Version.

In all scripture quotations, pronouns referring to God, Jesus or the Holy Spirit have been capitalised to align with the author's preference throughout the rest of the book.

Cover design by Jbooksdesign

Mary Swain
Website: www.maryswain.co.uk

This book is devoted to Dayspring Church.

To all the wonderful people of Dayspring, thank you for supporting me, encouraging me and cheering me on. Thank you for giving me a safe space to grow. I am so blessed to be part of such a joyful church family!

Praise for '40 Days of Delighting in God'

'Relevant – Inspiring – Challenging – Encouraging – Life-transformative.

40 days of Delighting in God is a collection of powerful reflections infused with meaningful questions with an invitation at the end of each chapter to dive deeper into intimacy with Jesus! Mary has a special gift of capturing in writing what God is saying, drawing on personal stories of application in her life, and engaging the reader in powerful personal reflection.

Mary's expressed hope is that you will have a greater revelation of His love, cherished moments of delighting in God and enjoy the adventure of hearing Him speak - that is certainly the impact in my life! But – only read one at a time or you'll miss the depth of treasure!'

Linda Harding – Advisor on international mission, mentor, coach, leader

'Mary draws from her own intimate walk with the Father, Son and Holy Spirit and her creativity to invite the reader in to deeper relationship with the God of the Bible. I recommend it with pleasure.'

Stuart Gregg – Kingdom Ministries and Celebrate School of Supernatural Ministry

'A devotional shouldn't just take you on an intellectual journey but a spiritual one that touches the depths of your spirit and soul. Mary in her devotional has invited the reader into a journey of a beautiful dance with Holy Spirit, Jesus and Father which increases intimacy. Mary writes with grace and integrity that will delight your soul and nourish your spirit.'

Liz Gregg – Kingdom Ministries and Celebrate School of Supernatural Ministry

Acknowledgements

Lee, thank you for your expert advice and for inspiring me to go for it!

Pippa, thank you for your meticulous and thorough proofreading.

Sharon, thank you for planting the seed that started me off on this book writing journey.

Suzi, thank you for being there for me, and for mentoring and encouraging me on the journey.

Dayspring Church, thank you for reading all my thoughts and musings over the last couple of years. Thank you for all your kind words which have spurred me on.

Mum and Dad, thank you for all your support and advice with this book. But mainly just thank you for being you. I am blessed to be called your daughter.

Most of all, thank you God for guiding me and strengthening me as I write. You're the best writing partner!

Contents

Introduction

One very ordinary day last year, I found myself sitting on my sofa with tears of joy pouring down my cheeks. Nothing in particular had happened, except that God came in and suddenly overwhelmed me with His love! I didn't see a vision or hear an audible voice. It was very unremarkable in one sense.

Yet, it has marked me ever since.

I just sat there and knew that God was with me. I felt so safe, so treasured and so engulfed in love. He just wanted me to know that I was His beloved.

I pray that as you read this book, you also might be marked by the cherished moments of delighting in God as He delights in you.

I pray that these reflections might open up a door to you having a greater revelation of His love for you.

I pray you might get to know Him on a deeper level and enjoy the adventure of hearing Him speak to you.

—————

There is no right way to read this book. You could read it consecutively over 40 days or you could dip in and out of it depending on which titles intrigue you in the moment!

However, I can recommend diving deep into the response sections. There is an invitation at the end of every devotion for you to take some time with God to reflect, to explore, to listen, and to delight in Him.

I often mention using your imagination to let God reveal to you what He wants to show you. Pictures, impressions and scenes in your imagination are some of the ways in which He can speak to us.

It can be tempting to think that by using your imagination, you are making it up. However, know that God created your imagination and your mind so He knows how to communicate with you through it. Often, it will be the first thing that comes into your head. If you are unsure, it is good to test what you hear against the Bible and what you know about God's character in it. God will never go against His Word and He is always good.

When I talk about listening to God, you may naturally lean more towards picturing or talking with either Father God, Jesus or Holy Spirit, and that's okay. They are all individual and all One!

It also would be a good idea to write down or draw what you see or hear in your encounters so that you can revisit them later for encouragement and strengthening. I often find that when I re-read something I've written, I can recognise how

God was speaking to me more than I could actually see it in the moment.

I invite you to take these reflections, prompts and questions as a starting point, but please do go on your own adventure with God and lean into what He is highlighting or revealing to you.

Let Him take the lead and delight in the journey!

A Joyful Invitation to Worship

'Worship the Lord with gladness; come before Him with joyful songs.'

Psalm 100:2

love springtime, when nature is bursting up from the ground with a multitude of colours, scents, and sounds. The trees are towering giants of vibrant green, each individual leaf dancing in the breeze. The flowers are like miniature, exquisite paintings all reflecting the glory of the painter. The whole of creation seems to be shouting out in complete awe of God!

When the crowds were joyfully praising Jesus as He came to Jerusalem as King on a donkey, He said, *'if they keep quiet, the stones will cry out.' (Luke 19:40)*

Creation will continue proclaiming the goodness of God even if we don't, but what a privilege and a joy it is that we have an invitation to join in with this worship!

I think worship is one of the most important things we can do in our lives. Powerful things happen when we worship that we can't always see with our eyes. When we worship, heaven and earth begin to beat with the same heartbeat. When we worship, our perspective shifts and we begin to see things through the lens of heaven, where Jesus has complete victory. This means things begin to come into alignment under Jesus in our spirit, our soul, our physical bodies and the environment around us.

Worship is also a weapon. It brings an atmosphere of victory that the enemy can't penetrate. Take a look at 2 Chronicles 20:21:

> *'Jehoshaphat appointed men to sing to the Lord and to praise Him for the splendour of His holiness as they went out at the head of the army.'*

In that situation, the battle was won while they were praising, and they didn't even need to start fighting!

Like that army, let's make worship our priority. Time spent in worship is never wasted time. It's good to intentionally set aside time for worship, whether that is singing, dancing, making music, delighting in God's presence in silence, or doing things like gardening, cooking and walking in nature. When these things are done with joyful attention on God, we are joining in the delightful dance of adoration and worship that is already happening all around us!

Set aside some time specifically for worship today. Get rid of anything that distracts you and purposefully turn your affections towards God. You could start by using your own words just to tell Him what you love about Him. Playing worship music is a great way to start, or if that's what you usually do, try worshipping God without any music!

What does it look like to do everyday tasks with joyful attention on Jesus? For example, what does it look like to worship while you are washing the dishes?

Are there things you can identify that draw you into a place of worship? For example, walking in nature, painting, writing, photography etc. Try intentionally making some time for these things.

Your Best Teacher

'But when He, the Spirit of truth, comes, He will guide you into all the truth.'

John 16:13

We are all different: all individually planned and known deeply by God because He took the time to make us.

So, because we are all different, the Holy Spirit is our best teacher. As a person of God who is living in us, He knows us better than anyone.

Imagine a classroom full of students. Each student is individual and learns in a different way, but the teacher delivers a lesson based on what is best for the class as a whole.

Now imagine a personal tutor in a one-to-one session. The tutor is able to tailor their lesson to suit the individual needs of the student. Both ways of learning are good, but the one-to-one session is more personal.

I like listening to different people teach from the Bible, and God has spoken to me immensely through the teaching of others. However, I found myself getting to a place where I was relying on others to hear the voice of God. It also led to some unhelpful comparisons with people who are at a different point in their journey from me.

All the while, I had a one-to-one tutor, the Holy Spirit, who was ready to teach me, strengthen me, guide me and chat with me, but I was settling for a second-hand message!

It can sometimes seem challenging or complicated to hear the voice of God, but remember that as someone who was hand-crafted by God, you are hardwired to hear His voice. You are fully known by Him, so He knows how best to communicate with you.

I love the description of Holy Spirit in the Amplified Bible:

> *'But the Helper (Comforter, Advocate, Intercessor – Counsellor, Strengthener, Standby), the Holy Spirit, whom the Father will send in My name [in My place, to represent Me and act on My behalf], He will teach you all things.' (John 14:26 AMP)*

So, please do learn from great teachers, but don't forget to listen to your best teacher, Holy Spirit!

✈ RESPONSE

Have a conversation with the Holy Spirit today. First, think of a situation or problem that you want to chat to Him about. Take some time to focus your attention on Him and then ask Him some specific questions about that situation.

Sometimes it's good to ask God to show you whatever He wants you to know, but other times I find it helpful to ask specific questions. You could try both!

Listen to His response. It will often be the first thing that comes into your head. It might come as a picture or a general impression. It's good to have a pen ready to write down what you see/hear.

Then revisit what you have written in a couple of days to see it with fresh eyes.

Giving Up or Laying Down?

'Suddenly an angel of the Lord appeared and a light shone in the cell. He struck Peter on the side and woke him up. "Quick, get up!" he said, and the chains fell off Peter's wrists.'

Acts 12:7

Peter was at the end of his road. Not only had he been put in prison, but he was grieving the loss of one of his closest friends, James, who had been killed by King Herod. It was the night before Peter's trial, and he was probably wondering whether like James, tomorrow he would also be put to death.

Yet suddenly, an angel of the Lord appeared and freed Peter from prison! It was a complete miracle!

Even though everything looked bleak for Peter, he wasn't praying or worshipping or crying out to God that night – he was sleeping. It seems a bit out of character for the fiery, active Peter.

There came a point for Peter where there was nothing he could do in his own strength to change the situation. It had to be through God's intervention, so Peter surrendered to God.

Surrender does not mean giving up. It means laying down. When you give up, you get hopelessness, but when you lay it down, you get peace.

Because Peter was fully yielded to God in this place of sleep, when the angel came, he could only do the very next step in front of him: what the angel told him to do.

This wasn't Peter's escape; it was God's deliverance. God's power was fully outworked through a surrendered Peter.

There are times when it's no use trying to fight or worry. The best thing to do is to lay it down. Surrender is an act of trust in God. Peter sleeping was him saying, "I trust you God whether you deliver me from prison or not."

Just before Jesus' death, Peter said he was ready to give up his life for Jesus, but these turned out to be empty words. However, throughout Acts, Peter learnt how to lay down his life as a living sacrifice, fully surrendered to the Holy Spirit's work within him.

For most of us, we won't have to give up our lives for the Gospel. But we are called to lay down our lives as a living sacrifice, because in our surrender, God's power can be fully realised.

Is there a place where you feel you are at the end of your road? Hold this before God and do a physical action of laying it down before Him. You're not giving up, you're placing it at His feet. Is there anything He wants to give you in return?

Are there dreams you have or promises over your life that you haven't seen come to pass yet? Do a physical action of laying them down before God as an act of trust and surrender to Him. Can you trust Him no matter what your circumstances look like?

Ask God to remind you of a time in your own life where He has been trustworthy. Write this down as something you can lean on.

The King of Glory

'Lift up your heads, you gates; lift them up, you
ancient doors, that the King of glory may come in.
Who is He, this King of glory? The Lord Almighty -
He is the King of glory.'

Psalm 24:9-10

Have you ever seen the film Aladdin? In the more recent
live action adaptation, there is a scene where 'Prince
Ali' enters the city, and it's one of the most extravagant
and over the top movie scenes I have ever seen!

There is an extremely long procession of dancers and musi-
cians all in colourful costumes, a whole zoo of animals, countless feathers, banners and confetti, and Prince Ali is riding on
top of a humongous elephant!

It makes me think of when the ark of the covenant was
brought into Jerusalem. In 2 Samuel 6:1, it says David brought

together 30,000 men! They entered Jerusalem with shouts and dancing and all sorts of musical instruments.

It would have been quite reasonable for David to be carried in amongst the procession. After all, he had just been promoted to king of Israel and all the people loved him.

Instead, David chose to give all the glory to God. He was on the ground, while the ark, the manifest presence of God, was being carried. He danced with all his might for 9 miles wearing a priest's garment, not his kingly robes. The extravagance was all for God: the one and only King of glory.

This then makes me think of Jesus entering Jerusalem as King. He could have organised a procession for himself and found a horse to ride on, but instead He came humbly on a donkey.

This is the King we serve: a King who meets us at our level. A servant King who models leadership by getting low and getting alongside us.

He will come again as King, this time with trumpets and angels, riding on the clouds, all powerful and radiating the fullness of the glory of God. The whole world will see that He is the Lord Almighty, the King of glory!

➤ RESPONSE

Picture Jesus returning in all His glory today. Take some time to ask questions, guided by the Holy Spirit. What does He look like? What does it sound like? What are the angels doing? What does seeing Him make you want to do?

> 'For the Lord Himself will come down from heaven, with a loud command, with the voice of the archangel and with the trumpet call of God, and the dead in Christ will rise first.' (1 Thessalonians 4:16)

Read this verse or any others similar verses you find and take some time to wonder at the coming of Jesus. We can't and won't know all the details now so we shouldn't get caught up in them, but taking some time to ponder all this can help us to learn something new about Jesus.

Beyond Measure

'"For My thoughts are not your thoughts, neither
are your ways My ways," declares the Lord.'

Isaiah 55:8

C an you measure out a kilogram of flour with a ruler?
Can you measure the length of a swimming pool with
some scales? Let me take you to one of Zechariah's
visions:

> 'Then I looked up, and there before me was
> a man with a measuring line in his hand. I
> asked, "Where are you going?" He answered
> me, "To measure Jerusalem, to find out how
> wide and how long it is." While the angel who
> was speaking to me was leaving, another an-
> gel came to meet him and said to him: "Run,
> tell that young man, 'Jerusalem will be a city

without walls because of the great number of
people and animals in it. And I Myself will be
a wall of fire around it,' declares the Lord, 'and
I will be its glory within." (Zechariah 2:1-5)

The man was trying to use a physical, earthy object to measure God's city. However, the important thing was not to measure the size of Jerusalem, but to consider the fact that God Himself will be the wall protecting it and God will be within it. Because the walls are made of fire, the city can grow and expand according to where God wants to move.

I wonder if we sometimes come to the kingdom of God with a big measuring stick and box it into tidy buildings and labels and Sunday mornings. But the kingdom of God is not something you can box in! It's wild and growing and often different from what we expect.

For the man with the measuring line, Jerusalem was so much bigger than he could even begin to comprehend in that moment. Sometimes, I think our dreams are too small in comparison to the greatness and power of God. I don't think we can out-dream God or surprise Him with how big our dreams are!

The fact that we can't measure the kingdom with earthly guides also means that small in the kingdom does not mean insignificant. We might be quick to disregard the small beginnings, the one-to-one conversations or the kitchen table gatherings, but these things are of such value to God.

So, let's not measure the things of the kingdom with our earthly guides. Let's widen our expectations of God and see things from heaven's perspective!

✐ RESPONSE

Ask God today where your dreams are too small compared to what He has in mind. Is there an area where God wants you to think bigger? What has made you think too small? Are you focussing on the natural resources or boundaries, or on God's kingdom? Ask God to give you kingdom vision when it comes to your dreams.

Ask God today where you might be disregarding the small things. Have you ever measured something, like a church or a business, by its numbers rather than its fruit? Ask God to show you the fruit of something that you might be judging by appearances.

Stick Together

'A friend loves at all times, and a brother is born for a time of adversity.'

Proverbs 17:17

We were never meant to do life alone. We were born out of a place of community – from a loving relationship between Father, Son and Holy Spirit. Because we were made in God's image, we were also designed to live in community with others.

We were made for life-giving friendships and relationships with other people just because we were made to love and be loved. It's not about what we can get out of relationships, but there is so much joy in having people to share with and do life with.

In the Bible it says we should carry each other's burdens *(Galatians 6:2)*, sharpen each other as iron sharpens iron *(Proverbs 27:17)*, share with each other *(Acts 2:44)*, encourage one another *(1 Thessalonians 5:11),* confess our sins to each other and pray for one other *(James 5:16).*

These things take vulnerability and mutual trust that can only be built by spending quality time with people and doing life together. Building lasting friendships in this biblical model is a slow but rewarding process.

There is a loneliness epidemic in the 21st century. It's easy to say that we need to find community and life-giving relationships, but it can be a lot harder to actually see that become a reality.

Our culture is becoming more and more wired towards surface level connections rather than deep and meaningful relationships. One of the biggest tactics of the devil is to isolate you because an isolated person is an easier target.

However, God knows our need for community. He is a God of miracles and nothing is too big for Him.

If we work with Him, He will guide us in the steps to take us deeper in our relationships. He will put people in our path that we enjoy spending time with and who we can mutually lean on for support.

God sees you and knows what you need!

Are there people in your life who are good friends where you can mutually depend and lean upon each other? Thank God for these people! What are the specific things that you want to thank God for in these people?

Are there friends in your life where you feel it would be good to get to know them more on a deeper level? Talk to God about these people. Is He prompting you be intentional in getting to know them more, and in what ways?

Do you feel you are lacking deep and meaningful relationships and friendships? Bring this before God and ask Him if there is anything He wants to say to you. Are there any actions you need to take? Is this something you could pray about regularly?

Peace that Surpasses Understanding

'Now may the Lord of peace Himself give you
peace at all times and in every way.'

2 Thessalonians 3:16

s it possible to be fully at peace? With countless worrying
news stories, is it even reasonable to have a sound mind? Is
it offensive to say that you are peaceful at a time like this?

I believe it is exactly in trying and testing moments when
we can experience *'the peace of God, which surpasses all understanding.' (Philippians 4:7 ESV)*

If everything was blue skies ahead, it wouldn't need to
surpass our understanding! It is in the midst of difficulty that
this peace of God becomes real and relevant.

Jesus said, *'I have told you these things, so that in Me you
may have peace. In this world you will have trouble. But take
heart! I have overcome the world.' (John 16:33)*

We will have trouble in this world. Peace doesn't mean getting rid of all the disruption – it means having a steadfast mind in the middle of it all because we know who God is. This peace comes from fixing our minds on Jesus because He is the 'Lord of peace.' (2 Thessalonians 3:16)

I think it takes faith and trust to believe that peace is ours, but it also takes proactivity to take hold of this peace. To take a slightly tangential example, in Psalm 73, the psalmist was envious and angry at another person. However, it was only when he entered God's presence that he gained perspective and clarity.

> 'Until I went into the sanctuary of God; then I
> discerned their end.' (Psalm 73:17 ESV)

In the sanctuary, in the presence of God, he could see things from God's viewpoint.

I believe this is true of many emotions we experience. If we are worried or anxious or uneasy, it is so easy to get caught up in these feelings, but when we enter into the presence of God, He brings clarity and peace. Spending time with God in the secret place means we become rooted in God and gain proper perspective: heaven's perspective. Peace is readily available to us if we choose to accept the invitation to abide in Him.

Jesus says, 'Peace I leave with you; My peace I give you.' (John 14:27)

We can experience peace, here and now: it's our inheritance!

Take a moment to still yourself. You might want to close your eyes. Focus on where Jesus is. He is already with you, but take some time to fix your attention on where He is. Linger there, just focusing on the Prince of Peace.

Imagine Jesus has a basket and He is inviting you to put into it anything you are worrying about. Put any worries in the basket, one by one. Watch and see what He does with the basket. Then ask Him if there is anything He wants to give you in return. Wait for His response. You may want to write it down afterwards.

Questions

> 'Then Philip ran up to the chariot and heard the
> man reading Isaiah the prophet. "Do you un-
> derstand what you are reading?" Philip asked.
> "How can I," he said, "unless someone explains
> it to me?"'
>
> Acts 8:30-31

In Acts 8, there is a wonderful story about Philip who bumps into a eunuch from Ethiopia on his travels. If you read the passage through, their whole conversation is entirely made up of questions!

Philip starts the conversation by asking the question, *'Do you understand what you are reading?'*. Then the eunuch replies, *'How can I, unless someone explains it to me?'*

Philip was brave in asking the question in the first place. He could have just carried on and ignored the eunuch, but instead he chose to say yes to the prompting of the Holy Spirit and start a conversation by asking a question.

It turned out to be an incredible encounter where he was able to tell the eunuch the good news of Jesus. It is amazing what God can do through someone stopping to ask a simple question.

The eunuch was also brave in asking his question. He was not afraid of looking inferior or damaging his reputation. He could have pretended that he understood what he was reading, but instead, he chose to ask for help.

Let's come to God and to others with our questions and let's not be embarrassed if we don't know something. In fact, let's even delight in finding questions which we don't know the answers to. I find myself more in awe of the greatness of God when I find things that are impossible for me to comprehend. If I understood everything, God wouldn't be God!

So, let's be like Philip and initiate conversations with questions and see where it leads.

Let's also be like the eunuch and not be afraid to ask questions about what we read or hear to deepen our understanding.

Let's also ask questions to God about Himself, knowing that we might not get all the answers, but knowing that we will get to know Him more on the journey.

➥ RESPONSE

Think of someone you might be meeting up with soon. Challenge yourself in that conversation to ask more questions rather than saying statements. Listen carefully to what the other person says so that it will raise more questions.

Is there something you have been wondering about in the Bible or about God recently? Bring that question to God and see what He might want to show you. It might help to write it down or draw a picture of what you see.

Is there someone you trust who you could take this question to? Often talking about things with others helps to bring clarity and a different perspective.

We Want a King!

> 'Of the greatness of His government and peace there will be no end. He will reign on David's throne and over his kingdom, establishing and upholding it with justice and righteousness from that time on and forever. The zeal of the Lord Almighty will accomplish this.'
>
> Isaiah 9:7

"We want a king!" cried Israel. Samuel was greatly distressed by this uproar. He knew that Israel was never meant to be led by a human king like the nations around them, but they were meant to be led by God.

'They have rejected Me as their King' (1 Samuel 8:7), the Lord said to Samuel.

"Hosanna in the highest" cried the people as they jumped and shouted, waving their palm branches as Jesus entered

Jerusalem as King on the donkey. But only five days later, the crowd rejected Jesus as King. "Crucify Him!" they screamed.

It was easy to praise Jesus along with the rest of the crowd having seen all the miracles He performed. But soon, it got difficult to praise.

Seeing Him arrested and tied up, bruised and battered, and silent before the Romans, it was no longer easy to praise. It was no longer convenient. This was not what they imagined.

So they rejected Him as King.

We have a history of wanting a king, but we also have a history of getting it wrong because we want a king made in our image. We want a convenient king. We want a popular king.

Jesus as King is not convenient for our man-made structures. Living in His kingdom under His rule and reign whilst on this earth will probably not make us popular. But He is victorious and undefeated. He is powerful and mighty. He is perfect and just.

We cry out for Jesus the King, but are we inviting Him into places and spaces where He has the freedom to be Himself? Or do we want Him to conform to our image and expectations?

There is no doubt of His kingdom coming. But Lord, help us work with You and not against You! Let us be partakers and not observers!

Come to God today with the line from the Lord's prayer:

> *'Your kingdom come, Your will be done, on earth as it is in heaven.' (Matthew 6:10)*

Speak this out loud a few times and meditate on each part of it and the meaning. Picture God before you as you say it. What does it look like for God's kingdom to come, here and now, where you live? What is God's will on earth as it is in heaven?

Ask God for forgiveness for where you might be wanting a king made in your own image. Ask God to help you to work with Him in His plans and purposes.

"Yes" to Jesus

'Whoever wants to be My disciple must deny themselves and take up their cross daily and follow Me.'

Luke 9:23

don't really like making decisions. Sometimes I just wish God would tell me exactly what to do and I'll do it! (At least I hope I would.) But Jesus is more relational than that. He's not a hard taskmaster and He loves to co-labour with us.

Sometimes when I'm faced with a decision, the most important choice to make first is just choosing to say yes to Jesus, no matter what.

It's always good to seek God's will with wisdom and discernment in decision making and it's something we should take seriously.

However, I've found that by first saying yes to Jesus, the original decision then carries less pressure and weight.

Sometimes it won't make things any clearer about what to choose, but a yes to Jesus sets your priorities straight and helps you see things from a kingdom perspective.

I've found that the most important thing in decision making is your overall attitude to following Jesus wholeheartedly, not necessarily the specific choice you make.

When you're in the kingdom, there isn't "one right thing" to do with your life. Often Jesus allows us to choose and might ask us, "What do you want to do?" The yes to Jesus is the one right way, and then there is joy in the journey of discovering and learning and co-labouring with Him.

We only need to say yes to Jesus once to be saved. However, it is also good to say yes to Jesus daily, just to live in that place of constant surrender to Him.

With Jesus as our Lord, our focus, our reason, and our example to follow, everything else will fall into place.

So next time you're faced with a decision to make, put the choice to one side for one second and make sure Jesus gets your first and biggest "yes"!

Do you have a decision to make? Take the decision and metaphorically hold it in your hands. How does it feel when you hold it? Does it feel heavy?

Now picture Jesus in front of you. Place the decision down so you can take hold of Jesus' hands with both of your hands. Say "yes" to Him when you are ready.

Then go back and pick up the decision. Focus on Jesus as you weigh it in your hands. What do you feel Jesus is saying to you?

Could you make a daily routine of saying "yes" to Jesus every morning?

Let It Approach

'The plan of the Holy One of Israel—let it approach, let it come into view, so we may know it.'

Isaiah 5:19

Imagine there is a car on the horizon driving towards you. You might be able to make out the rough outline, but you wouldn't be able to see any details. Then as it comes closer, you might be able to see the colour more clearly, and then the structure of the car, taking a guess at the make. Only when it gets much closer would you be able to read the number plate and see the badge on the front.

This image reflects what it looks like to let the plans of God approach and come into view. We might be able to see a glimmer of something on the horizon and describe its general qualities, but we don't know any of the intricacies. We must wait and let it approach before we can start to see more of the details.

I often have a tendency to want to know everything right now! But if we knew everything now, it might not make sense in our current context, or we might try and run with it in our own strength too early.

Things will become apparent in time; we just need to be patient.

It's important that we learn to be content in the season that we're currently in. I believe it's good to look ahead to the future and to dream with God, but this is not where we should live. We need to live in the present. If we live in the future (or in the past), we will miss out on the good gifts that God has for us in the current moment.

I think being content in the season we're in looks like taking things slowly, appreciating the small things, being thankful, recognising opportunities when they arise, and purposefully finding joy in our everyday.

God's timing is always perfect. He's never late, never early, and always right on time. We need to learn to walk in step with His rhythms for this current season.

Take some time to have a chat with God. Ask Him, what season am I in right now? Ask Him to show you the characteristics of the season.

Ask Him, what rhythm are You playing right now that I need to get in step with? Is it fast or slow? A steady pulse or syncopated? Accelerating or decelerating? Ask God to show you what this rhythm means and how you can begin to synchronise with it in this season. Can you tap out the rhythm?

Also, take some time to look out to the horizon and dream. Ask God to show you something new about the next season and write it down/draw it. Delight in the excitement and anticipation of the next season whilst dwelling in the present.

One Thing

'One thing I ask from the Lord, this only do I seek:
that I may dwell in the house of the Lord all the
days of my life, to gaze on the beauty of the Lord
and to seek Him in His temple.'

Psalm 27:4

The verse above is my favourite Bible verse. I love speaking
it out to God as a prayer.

We can pray so many different prayers and God
loves it when we speak with Him about all kinds of things that
are going on. We might pray for a friend or family member, for
something we see going on in the news, for help with decision
making etc.

All these are great prayers, but is there one that is the most
important?

David's number one prayer was for the presence of God. The 'one thing' David desired was God Himself, not what God could do. His priority was presence.

We must learn to live in this place of pure relationship with God just because of who He is. We must learn what it means to dwell.

When it comes to the presence of God and worship, we so often get a quick fix and move on. But to dwell in the house of the Lord means abiding, waiting, communing, residing and being.

It's not always easy to dwell in God's presence with no agenda. In our driven culture it can feel unproductive. But time spent in the presence of God is never wasted time.

Even if we don't feel anything in particular or gain any revelation or insight, just being with God is the priority. In His presence is the fullness of life.

I don't think dwelling in the house of the Lord means camping out in a church building 24/7, but I think it means living life at Jesus' feet, seeking to be more aware of His presence day by day, hour by hour and minute by minute.

Then everything we do will stem from this place of abiding.

I know that I want this to be my number one prayer too: my 'one thing'.

Speak out Psalm 27:4 to God as a prayer. Try changing the parts where it says 'Lord' to 'You' to make it more personal:

> *'One thing I ask of You, this only do I seek: that I may dwell in Your house all the days of my life, to gaze upon Your beauty and to seek You in Your temple.'*

What do you notice as you speak it out? Is there a particular part of the verse that stands out to you? What does it look like to dwell in the house of the Lord? What does it look like to gaze upon His beauty? What does it look like to seek Him?

Is there another verse that means a lot to you that you could speak out as a prayer to God? Why not make a daily habit of it?

Living Stones

'As you come to Him, the living Stone—rejected
by humans but chosen by God and precious to
Him—you also, like living stones, are being built
into a spiritual house to be a holy priesthood,
offering spiritual sacrifices acceptable to God
through Jesus Christ.'

1 Peter 2:4-5

When people come together in unity, there is
strength. Standing together in agreement about
something is powerful. However, real and last-
ing strength comes from being built on the Cornerstone: Jesus.
True strength and complete unity can only be attained when
everything is measured from, lined up with and built on Him.
Our strength lies in the strength of the Cornerstone, which is
beyond compare.

I've never built a stone wall, but this image of us being
living stones fitted together intrigued me. In a stone wall, each

stone is supporting another stone whilst simultaneously being supported by the stones underneath. A drystone wall only works because each stone is a bit different, which means they can fit together with more traction. Some flatter stones are used to line the edges, longer ones are used to span the width of the wall and smaller ones fill in the gaps. All the different shapes and sizes are needed.

The cornerstone is the very first stone that is laid and from it comes the measuring line and the plumb line. It has to be the best stone – one with no imperfections that could compromise the structure. It is a pure stone, creating a strong foundation and base for everything else.

Paul says, *'From Him the whole body, joined and held together by every supporting ligament, grows and builds itself up in love, as each part does its work.' (Ephesians 4:16)*

The key is that we are held together because of Jesus. From Him we find proper order and absolute truth.

There are so many different traditions and ways of doing things in churches that we could easily get caught up in our differences. But when it's all about Him and not all about us, that is where our strength as the body of Christ lies. Then our differences don't have to be destructive stumbling blocks, but different expressions can be celebrated. If our focus is on "the right way" to do things, we will crumble. But if our focus is on Him, we will be united under Jesus.

Ask God to show you a picture of Jesus as the Cornerstone. What do you notice about His strength, His shape and His placement? What can you learn about Him from this?

Next time you get chance, go out and have a look at a brick or stone wall. What do you notice about how it is built? What do you notice about the individual stones or bricks? What does God want to say to you in relation to what you notice about the wall? Ask Him to show you what it looks like for us to be living stones built together.

Do you ever find yourself caught up in differences that lead to division or judgement? Bring this before God and ask Him what He wants to say about this.

Childlike Faith

'Truly I tell you, unless you change and become like little children, you will never enter the kingdom of heaven.'

Matthew 18:3

There's a difference between being childish and childlike. The former is more like the opposite of maturity. The Bible talks about us moving on from milk onto solid food in our faith, so it's important that we learn and grow in maturity, seeking a deeper understanding of the Word and applying it to our lives so that we don't remain the same as when we first accepted Christ.

However, I think being childlike is something completely different to being childish. It's about having a faith in which there is complete trust in God and purity in relationship with Him. There is no kind of over-complication, suspicion or offence.

I love working with children because they haven't learnt any of the supposed "rules". They haven't got any of the blockages to encountering Jesus that we often unknowingly gain as we grow up. There is a beautiful simplicity to their faith. They embrace Jesus and the gifts of the Holy Spirit as second nature.

Practically speaking, what does it mean for us to be childlike in our relationship with God?

For me, I think it looks like daily surrender to His love, sitting with Him with no agenda, having a laugh with God, and doing things I enjoy just to delight and have fun.

I love dancing in particular, and it has invited a new sense of childlikeness into my relationship with God. I do feel that as my physical body lets go into freedom, so does my spirit. Being childlike might look completely different for you.

Being childlike is also embracing how our Father sees us. He delights in us more than we could ever imagine and rejoices over us!

Let's accept and rest in this knowledge with a childlike trust. Let's take God at His word – when He says He loves us, there is no question about it!

🕊 RESPONSE

Picture yourself as a child with your Father God. Use your imagination to explore this. Maybe you want to sit on His lap and hear His heartbeat. Maybe He wants to tell you a story! Does He want to dance with you? Does He want to take you on an adventure? Delight in letting this adventure with Father God unfold.

Picturing yourself as a child or with Father God can be difficult, especially if you have experienced trauma as a child or have a difficult relationship with your parents.

If this is the case, is there somebody you trust that you could talk to about this? Talking things through with a trusted friend, mentor or partner, as well as journeying with God, can bring healing and freedom.

In All Your Ways

'Trust in the Lord with all your heart, and do not lean on your own understanding. In all your ways acknowledge Him, and He will make straight your paths.'

Proverbs 3:5-6 (ESV)

I have been struck by how many times in the Gospel of John, Jesus emphasises that He can do nothing apart from the Father. Jesus, although He is fully God, limited Himself whilst on earth and only acted out of relationship and in response to what the Father was doing.

This is good news for us because Jesus has given us an example that we can follow! If He did not limit Himself, we would be in awe of the things He did, but wouldn't think it was anything we could do.

Yet Jesus said, *'whoever believes in Me will do the works I have been doing, and they will do even greater things than these, because I am going to the Father.' (John 14:12)*

With Holy Spirit as our guide, we can follow Jesus' example and do even greater things. It's what He says!

> *'In all your ways acknowledge Him, and he will make straight your paths.' (Proverbs 3:6)*

In all His ways, Jesus acknowledged the Father, so how much more should we do that!

The Hebrew word for 'acknowledge' is translated as 'know' for the majority of other times it appears in the Old Testament. It's through relationship and getting to know God that we can understand His ways and walk in the paths He has for us.

The NIV version of this verse is, *'In all your ways submit to Him.'*

Submission is often seen as a negative thing because it has connotations of weakness. But in submission to the Father, we are strong! We are not emptied of ourselves; we are filled up with Him! We haven't lost our dreams or direction; we are filled up with God's dreams! God's desires become our true desires, and that is a beautiful place to be.

The verse continues with, *'He will make straight your paths.'* When we are filled up with the knowledge of who God is and who we are in Him, we can walk with freedom and confidence in the paths He has carved out for us.

Consider this verse:

> *'Whoever believes in Me will do the works I have been doing, and they will do even greater things than these, because I am going to the Father.' (John 14:12)*

How do you feel about what Jesus has said here? Think of some of the things Jesus did. With the Holy Spirit living in you, do you believe you can do these things too?

The next time you have the opportunity to pray with someone, take a second to stop and ask God what He is doing. Don't jump in straight away with what you think you should pray. What you think may not be wrong, but it's good practice to take a breath and notice what God wants to do. How can you join in with what He is doing?

A Living Testimony

'Let your light shine before others, that they may see your good deeds and glorify your Father in heaven.'

Matthew 5:16

Jesus is really good news for all people.

One day, I was out on the streets with a team who were offering to pray for people as they went about their day.

I chatted with a Hindu man who had a couple of health issues and was on his way to find a new job, so he was really appreciative that we were offering prayer. After praying with him for those things, he said, "What I really want is peace because I worry a lot."

I had a Bible in my bag, so I showed him a couple of verses that talk about peace in Jesus. As he read the verses, what he said really struck me: "Even the Hindu priests and those highest up have so much worry on their faces. But what is written here about peace, it looks like this is a reality for you. It looks like you actually have peace."

This both encouraged me but also challenged me. What he said was true – I do have peace because of the Prince of Peace. But it also challenged me because it made me realise that people watch and take note of how we live and act. It reminded me of this verse in Acts:

> *'They were astonished and they took note that*
> *these men had been with Jesus.' (Acts 4:13)*

As those who have spent time with Jesus, we have the privilege of representing Him to the people around us so that they might know Jesus for themselves. So, I was challenged to be as good a representation of Jesus as possible!

Let's abide in God's presence and in Jesus' teachings so that we might be a living example of the truth and power of the Word. Let's go out in confidence and assurance so that we can be a walking testimony of the good news of Jesus.

So, *'live as children of light' (Ephesians 5:8)* and *'let your light shine before others, that they may see your good deeds and glorify your Father in heaven'! (Matthew 5:16)*

Go and stand in front of a mirror. Imagine that in the reflection, instead of yourself, you can see Jesus. Ask Him to show you, in what ways are you a reflection of Jesus? What do you carry that are characteristics of Jesus?

Ask God to show you what it looks like when your light shines. When does your light shine brightest? What does your light look like as you walk down the street? What does it look like as you have conversations with others? What is bright about you?

Is there any way in which you might be hiding your light? Have a conversation with God about it.

God-Confidence

'What I have said, that I will bring about; what I
have planned, that I will do.'

Isaiah 46:11

wonder, is it possible to be fully confident about anything?

I think that depends on where we put our confidence.
I think we can only really be fully confident if we place our
confidence entirely in God.

God always keeps His word. We often don't because we
forget or we change our mind, but God is not like that. We know
from the Bible that *'no word from God will ever fail.' (Luke 1:37)*

When God says something, it is impossible for nothing
to happen.

> *'So is My word that goes out from My mouth:*
> *It will not return to Me empty, but will accom-*
> *plish what I desire and achieve the purpose for*
> *which I sent it.' (Isaiah 55:11)*

As believers, I think we should be the most confident people around. Hopefully not because we have an inflated ego, but because we know where to put our confidence.

When we put our confidence in God, in His promises and what He has said in His Word, we don't rely on our own performance or ability, but on God's unmatched and unmeasurable ability. We therefore shouldn't get too caught up in our mistakes or weaknesses, because what is that in comparison to God's power?

When we put our confidence in God, we don't need to try and muster up great levels of faith on our part. We can simply place it all in the more than capable hands of God and let Him work in and through us.

Our faith is in Him, not in ourselves. The weight is all on Jesus, but He can handle it all because He has overcome the world.

There is no power that is greater and no god that can exceed His magnitude. So, we can remain fully confident because our confidence is in God and in His Word! That the safest place to put our trust.

Do you have promises over your life from God that you personally have received? Have you written them down? If not, write them down now.

Have you ever explored some the promises of God that are written in the Bible? When you are reading the Bible, try highlighting the promises of God as you come across them or search for some and make a list.

Take a look at God's promises over you: ones you have received personally or ones in the Bible that are for all believers. Look at each one. How do you feel about it? Do you feel confident about it or unsure? As you read each promise, speak out the words of Mary, the mother of Jesus, if you feel ready:

'May Your word to me be fulfilled.' (Luke 1:38)

Set Apart for the King

'In a palace you find many kinds of containers and
tableware ... some of them are used for banquets
and special occasions, and some for everyday
use. But you, Timothy, must not see your life and
ministry this way. Your life and ministry must not
be disgraced, for you are to be a pure container
of Christ and dedicated to the honourable purposes of your Master, prepared for every good
work that He gives you to do. Run as fast as you
can from all the ambitions and lusts of youth; and
chase after all that is pure. Whatever builds up
your faith and deepens your love must become
your holy pursuit.'

2 Timothy 2:20-22 TPT

Paul talks about containers. In the Old Testament, containers and other objects were either holy (used in the
tabernacle/temple) or common (for everyday use). The

same went for people. All the people were common, but the priests and Levites were holy. There was nothing wrong with being common, but the priests were set apart from the rest to minister to God on behalf of the people.

We know from 1 Peter 2:9 that we are *a chosen people, a royal priesthood, a holy nation, God's special possession*. We are all priests, qualified by Jesus and washed clean by Him. By His blood we are holy and set apart for the King. It's not something we need to achieve, but it's who we are.

Because we are set apart for the King, we should not look like the rest of the world. Esther was set apart for the king and after her 12 months of beauty treatments I imagine she looked different to the other women outside the palace! Daniel and his friends were set apart for the king and I imagine they also looked, sounded and acted differently after training in the king's palace for 3 years. We should also be distinguishable from the world around us because we are living in the kingdom of God.

Going back to containers, it's not enough just to empty ourselves of the *'ambitions and lusts of youth'*, but we must be filled up with the things of Christ. Otherwise, we're just left with empty space! We must be filled up with the Word of God in our hearts and God's thoughts in our heads. This is our training and our beauty treatment - our *'holy pursuit'*!

So, we *are* set apart and made holy by the blood of Jesus. That is who we are and there's nothing we can do to make ourselves more clean or holy. But we are also *called* to be set apart in the way we look, think and act in the communities around us.

✒ RESPONSE

Take some time to meditate on the verse below and the fact that Jesus' blood has made you clean and holy. You are chosen and set apart for Him.

> 'We have been made holy through the sacrifice of the body of Jesus Christ once for all.'
> (Hebrews 10:10)

What does it look like for you to be distinguishable from the world around you? Is there a situation in your family or work life, for example, when you can consciously choose differently from those around you? It might be something like speaking positive words when there is gossip or choosing honesty when others may be lying. It may be something that is costly. Ask God how you are called to be set apart.

No Parachutes Needed!

> 'But those who hope in the Lord will renew their strength. They will soar on wings like eagles; they will run and not grow weary, they will walk and not be faint.'
>
> Isaiah 40:31

When Jesus was talking to Nicodemus, he says, *'The wind blows wherever it pleases. You hear its sound, but you cannot tell where it comes from or where it is going. So it is with everyone born of the Spirit.'* (John 3:8)

We need to be alert to where the wind is blowing – where the Spirit is moving. We might not understand it fully, but because we have God's Spirit in us, we can recognise the wind, catch it, and fly with it.

I love the image of us flying with God. Like an eagle, we can soar effortlessly on the thermals, catching the wind. Eagles don't need any kind of parachute or safety net when they fly, and neither do we when flying with God.

Parachutes are good things that help us stay in control when falling. But we are not falling, we're flying! We're not going downwards; we're going onwards and upwards. Having a parachute would actually be a hindrance when trying to fly!

If we want to fly with God, there is an invitation to get rid of anything that is distracting us or hindering us from flying with full freedom and complete focus on God.

When David went to fight Goliath, he couldn't wear Saul's armour because even though armour is a good thing, it wasn't right for David, and it was actually a hindrance to him. With God, he had all the protection he needed.

With God, we have everything we need to fly. So let us throw off everything that hinders us from soaring!

The things that you need to leave behind or take with you into the next season might be different to other people, but seek God about it because He knows what's right for you. He'll guide you and fly with you, but you might need to take a leap of faith first!

Picture yourself standing on the edge of a cliff with Jesus. Is He inviting you to fly with Him? How do you feel about that?

Take a look at yourself. Is there anything you are holding on to or anything you are dressed in that is not suitable for flying? Ask Jesus about it. Is He asking you to let go of it or take it off? You might need to take some time to let it go.

Imagine yourself taking a leap off the cliff and soaring like an eagle with Jesus. How does it feel? What is the look on His face as you fly together?

More Boldness

'For I am not ashamed of the gospel, because
it is the power of God that brings salvation to
everyone who believes.'

Romans 1:16

Peter, full of the Holy Spirit, spoke incredibly boldly about
Jesus in front of the Jewish leaders in Acts 4. He had
just been put in jail for sharing the good news, but even
when standing before the very people who killed Jesus, he did
not hold back. The crazy thing is, a few verses later he is on his
knees praying for more boldness!

> *'Now, Lord, consider their threats and enable
> your servants to speak Your word with great
> boldness.' (Acts 4:29)*

The Greek word for boldness here also translates as speaking plainly and openly. Speaking boldly about Jesus doesn't

mean shouting. It doesn't correlate with the number of people you're speaking to. It just means being honest and speaking truth. It can take a lot of boldness just to speak to one person about the truth of Jesus Christ.

I have been on a journey of sharing my faith with others. When I was at school, I rarely told anyone I was a Christian because I was scared of what people might think. But gradually as I grew in my relationship with Jesus, I became more and more open about my faith because the love of Jesus just overflowed.

Now, I enjoy having conversations about my faith. I don't speak loudly or put on a particular voice, but I just try and share as openly and plainly as I can. I try not to hide or sugarcoat anything. Jesus is absolute truth and He is the reason for my everything, so it would not be authentic for me to try and hide that! Often just pure honesty raises intrigue.

Have you ever noticed how if you speak the name of Jesus in a conversation, the atmosphere changes? It's almost as though the name of Jesus just demands a response. If we talk about God, it seems less specific, but when we speak the name of Jesus, it suddenly becomes personal and real. So, let's name drop Jesus all over our conversations!

When the opportunities arise, let's speak boldly by being open, honest and truthful about Jesus Christ. Jesus is not ashamed to call us brothers and sisters, so let's unashamedly proclaim His name!

What does speaking boldly look like for you? After reading this, what do you feel God's invitation is to you?

Next time an opportunity comes up to speak about your faith, challenge yourself to use the name of Jesus. It's good to try and avoid using Christian jargon and exclusive words and phrases, but for example, if you mention that you went to church, be specific about what you did at church or what you particularly enjoyed.

Is there a testimony you have that you can share? What has God done for you recently that you could tell someone about?

Don't Take My Word For It!

'Taste and see that the Lord is good.'

Psalm 34:8

magine that somebody comes up to you and says, "I tried this new chocolate bar and it's the best thing I've ever tasted!" Would you just take their word for it? Would you just say, "That's nice. Glad you enjoyed it." No! You'd want to try it for yourself!

Now let's imagine someone saying to you, "God is good!" Don't just take their word for it! I don't mean be cynical and not believe them, but just don't settle for someone else's experience.

The Bible says, *'Taste and see that the Lord is good.'* *(Psalm 34:8)*

David urges us to seek God and experience His goodness for ourselves with that first-hand, experiential and personal knowledge of tasting.

In John 1, Philip tells Nathanael about Jesus and how He is the Messiah that the prophets wrote about. When Nathanael has questions, Philip says, *'Come and see.' (John 1:46)*

Philip urged Nathanael not just to take his word for it, but to actually come and see Jesus and experience who He is for himself. Then Nathanael has a personal encounter with Jesus where Jesus spoke powerfully into His life!

There is a time for standing in faith and taking God at His word. But so often, we settle for a second-hand experience of the kingdom.

We hear people speak about powerful encounters with God and the miraculous breaking out, but we settle with just taking their word for it. Maybe we fully believe them, but we don't hunger for it to happen where we are.

I think sometimes we can be quick to put up barriers by saying things like, "Well they're much more spiritual than me," or, "They're in a different part of the world." But God does not put up these barriers. The things of the kingdom that Jesus paid for are open to all.

How hungry are you to taste the goodness of God and all that His kingdom offers? Don't take someone else's word for it. Experience it for yourself!

What are you hungry for? Is there something that you've heard about, for example, seeing healing or the miraculous, that you want to taste for yourself? Bring it before God. Ask Him if there is a key to seeing this in a greater measure that you need to take hold of.

In your imagination, ask God to show you His goodness. Visualise God giving you His goodness to taste. What does it look like? As you eat it, what does it taste like? Is it sweet? Is it rich? What else does He want to show you about His goodness? Write/draw what you see/hear.

What's Your Response?

'In the time of those kings, the God of heaven will set up a kingdom that will never be destroyed, nor will it be left to another people. It will crush all those kingdoms and bring them to an end, but it will itself endure forever.'

Daniel 2:44

Known as 'Herod the Great', King Herod ruled over Judea in the 1st century BC with his 'Herodian kingdom'. He was favoured by the Romans, was given the title 'King of Judea', and was appointed to keep the peace in the area. Known for his extravagant building projects, he was powerful, prosperous, and thriving.

Yet he was disturbed by a baby.

> 'When King Herod heard this he was disturbed.' (Matthew 2:3)

Not only disturbed, but he turned to desperate measures when he ordered all the boys under 2 to be killed in Bethlehem! How could the news of one baby cause him to commit this horrific act?

After the Magi had visited Herod wanting to worship Jesus, Herod called the Jewish leaders together to find out exactly what was happening. The Jewish leaders knew the scriptures well, so they told Herod about the prophecies of the coming King.

I can imagine them saying, "Oh yes, there's a lot written about Him. This is a big deal. It says the Messiah will be born in Bethlehem, near here! It says in the book of Daniel that God will have a kingdom that will never be destroyed and it will crush all the other kingdoms."

Herod must have been quaking in his boots! He was the 'King of Judea'! His 'Herodian kingdom' surely could not be crushed!

Herod was greatly disturbed because all he had worked for and established was being threatened. With the coming of a King whose kingdom would never end, he would have to lay down his own kingdom. If this baby really is the Messiah and if all the prophecies are true, there will be no room for any other kings!

As a tiny baby was born in a stable in Bethlehem, Herod, the Jewish leaders, the Magi, the shepherds and probably the sheep too were all quaking. Some in excitement, some in fear, some in awe, some in anger, some in wonder. The birth of

Jesus Christ meant everything would change forever. Some responded in a good way and others in a destructive way. Either way, His birth demands a response. What's yours?

✍ RESPONSE

Take a moment to place yourself in the story of Jesus' birth. You might want to read the story in Luke 2 first. Imagine you are one of the visitors who is there to see Jesus. What do you see, hear, smell and feel as you enter the stable? Can you see Jesus? What do you feel as you see Him? With the knowledge that He is God, here as a tiny baby, what is your response to Him?

Think of some of the things in your life that you do/places that you go to. If these things disappeared tomorrow, how would you feel? It would be normal to feel disappointed and lost, but it is good to ask yourself this question to see where your values and priorities lie. Is there any material thing you are grasping onto too tightly or feel too protective over?

Choose Your Words Wisely

'The tongue has the power of life and death.'

Proverbs 18:21

We've all probably heard the question, "If you were given X amount of money, what would you do with it?" I would like to pose a different question with a similar theme.

What would you say if you only had 100 words to speak?

Let's say you are spending the evening with family or friends, but you could only speak 100 words for the whole evening: how would you spend them? Would you talk about yourself? Would you use them to encourage someone else in the room? Would you gossip? Would you speak about Jesus?

It's a hypothetical situation, but I imagine that if we knew we only had a limited number of words to use, we would consider what we say much more carefully.

In Colossians 4:6, Paul says *'Let your conversation be gracious and attractive.'* NLT (I like the New Living Translation here).

What kinds of conversations are attractive to heaven? The ones that build each other up; the ones that are loving; the ones where there is listening; the ones full of hope.

Your words are very powerful. You have the opportunity to choose to speak peace or hope into someone's situation. You have the opportunity to be gracious and merciful when a person may be expecting anger. You have the opportunity to speak well of someone when others might be putting them down.

We can also use our words to make declarations over ourselves or into the environment around us. I believe this has much more power than we might initially see.

As children of God, we have been given *'authority to trample on snakes and scorpions and to overcome all the power of the enemy.' (Luke 10:19)* One way in which we activate this authority is through our words.

We can partner with God or partner with the enemy in what we say, even unknowingly. So, let's choose partner with God by speaking words of life, truth and hope!

Remember, there is no law against love, joy, peace, patience, kindness, goodness, faithfulness, gentleness and self-control! (*Galatians 5:22-23*) Which of these fruits of the Spirit do you want to see more in your conversations? Have a chat to God about what this looks like.

Are you aware of anything you may have been speaking over yourself or others that is limiting or destructive? Ask God to reveal anything to you that you might not be aware of. Ask God what he wants you to speak out instead. It would be a good idea to write down what He says and speak those things over yourself as declarations. You might have different declarations for different seasons.

The Undignified Father

> 'But while he was still a long way off, his father saw him and was filled with compassion for him; he ran to his son, threw his arms around him and kissed him.'
>
> Luke 15:20

There is nothing better than the Father's love. He takes great delight in you and rejoices over you. He is slow to anger but abounding in love. He loves to spend time with you and He beams with joy when He sees you.

In Jesus' parable about the prodigal son, my favourite part of the story is the father's response. As soon as he realised the son was coming back, he went out to meet him – and he didn't just walk, he ran!

This was all before high rise buildings, so when the father saw the son *a long way off* and started out to meet him, he could have been running for miles!

It was also pretty shameful to run in Middle Eastern culture, especially for an older man and the head of the house. He probably would have had to hitch up his tunic in order to run which would have been seen as pretty undignified.

But the father was determined to meet his son with nothing other than extravagant love, no matter the cost.

I also like that in the following verses when the son says, *'I am no longer worthy to be called your son,'* the father doesn't answer him or try to correct him, but he says *'Quick!'* and just showers him with love and blessings.

He doesn't just *tell* the son how much he loves him and how he is worthy to be called his son, but he *shows* him through extravagant love.

I once heard someone share a picture of how God is laughing and crying with joy and love and compassion over His children. I think that's how I imagine the father in this story – crying and laughing all at once over the younger son as he runs to him and hugs him.

The Father's love is immeasurable and utterly transformative!

Read the story of the prodigal son in Luke 15:11-32. As you do, focus on the father and take note of anything that stands out to you. Is this image of the father in line with how you see Father God? What is the same or different? If there is anything that is different between the father in the story and how you see Father God, ask God to reveal to you the truth of what He is like.

Take some time today to delight in Father God's love and presence. In your imagination, ask Him to show you a picture of what His love looks like. Ask God for a deeper revelation of that love at the very core of your being.

Remaining Faithful

'For though we live in the world, we do not wage war as the world does.'

2 Corinthians 10:3

Reflecting on the book of Daniel, I have been amazed at how a whole nation was turned around just because of Daniel's faithfulness to God.

In Daniel 6, King Darius was persuaded to issue a decree where no one was allowed to pray to anyone except himself for 30 days, otherwise they would be thrown into the den of lions. You might have heard the story: Daniel did pray to God, got thrown into the lions' den, and God rescued him.

But I think the truly amazing thing is that King Darius then wrote a letter to *'all the nations and peoples of every language in all the earth' (Daniel 6:25)* saying that everyone must fear and reverence God. This is followed by a song of praise!

Imagine a significant leader who previously did not follow God then testifying to the goodness of God before the whole world and writing Him a song of praise!

There was a major turnaround for the king and the whole nation, just because Daniel prayed.

In Daniel 6:10, it says, *'Three times a day he got down on his knees and prayed, giving thanks to his God, just as he had done before.'*

He didn't loudly protest at the palace or try and fight back. Instead, he trusted the matter completely to God and his protest was continuing to pray every day.

He also did not give in to fear because by praying by his open window, he didn't try to hide the fact that he served God. He just simply and quietly remained faithful.

There's lots more to the story but in essence, because Daniel stayed true to God when the world around him was changing, God used him to cause a significant shift in the nation.

There is a time to stand up and speak, but there is also a time to get down on our knees and pray. Maybe there's a situation where the best way to take action is just to remain faithful to God in the midst of change around us. In Daniel's case, it turned around a nation.

Ask God if there may be an area where you might have come under the enemy's broadcast of fear or hopelessness recently. Ask God to take you higher and picture yourself being lifted up and above the clouds where things are clear. How do you feel as you are lifted higher?

> 'And God raised us up with Christ and seated
> us with Him in the heavenly realms in Christ
> Jesus.' (Ephesians 2:6)

Ask God to show you what it looks like for you to be seated in heavenly places. Ask Him to show you your seat. Imagine sitting in it. How does it feel to be seated here? What does it mean for you to be seated here whilst still living in the world?

Happy to See You

'The Lord your God is with you, the Mighty Warrior who saves. He will take great delight in you; in His love He will no longer rebuke you, but will rejoice over you with singing.'

Zephaniah 3:17

How do you perceive God when you come into His presence? Is He happy to see you? Does He want to speak to you?

When I come into God's presence, I can sometimes come under the false impression that because I haven't heard anything from Him straight away or I can't sense Him near me, that God doesn't want to speak to me right now or I must have done something wrong. Let's just laugh at that lie, shall we!

He's always happy to see us and delighted to speak with us, no matter how we might be feeling. God is in a good mood!

When the prodigal son was ashamed to face his father, the father was overwhelmed with joy just to see his son! He didn't see his mistakes, he just saw his precious, beloved son.

God is always pleased to welcome us into His presence and He has things that He wants to share with us.

There's no formula to somehow unlock hearing His voice. We hear His voice by grace, not by merit on our part. It's not a test that we have to pass or a level that we have to reach.

Especially if we're feeling down or have made a bad decision, it's all the more important that we don't let this become a barrier between us and God because of any subtle condemnation that we place on ourselves.

God loves spending time with us more than we like spending time with Him! His disposition towards us is favourable and loving. He loves to partner with us and share His heart with those He trusts.

In the verse at the beginning, it says God takes delight in us and rejoices over us. He sings and leaps and spins around with joy when He sees you!

Have you ever pictured God rejoicing over you with singing? Why not ask Him today to show you what that looks like?

When you come to pray, how do you picture God? Next time you come to pray, picture either Father God, Jesus or the Holy Spirit with you in your room. Or all three! Where are they? What are they doing?

If you ever feel condemnation or a barrier that is pulling you away from entering into God's presence, speak out this verse:

> 'In Him and through faith in Him we may
> approach God with freedom and confidence.'
> (Ephesians 3:12)

Sorting Out Your Post

'Therefore, since we are surrounded by such a great cloud of witnesses, let us throw off everything that hinders and the sin that so easily entangles. And let us run with perseverance the race marked out for us.'

Hebrews 12:1

When you get post through your letterbox, you need to sort through it. There may be some things, like a letter of encouragement from a friend, that you keep and revisit. Then there are important letters which require action - you have to deal with them at some point or they may cause more problems down the line. Then there are flyers and advertisements – if they are not useful to you, you sift them out of the pile and throw them away so they don't cause clutter.

I wonder whether God is inviting us to take a bit of time to "sort through our post" in relation to keeping in step with God's plans and purposes.

What things are you going to choose to hold on to for encouragement and comfort?

We need to soak in the Word of God, for *'all Scripture is God-breathed and is useful for teaching, rebuking, correcting and training in righteousness.' (2 Timothy 3:16)*

We need to hold on to God's promises and stand on answered prayers and testimonies that raise our faith.

What things do you need to take some time to deal with and then move on from? Maybe there's an action you need to take before letting something go, like forgiving someone or asking for forgiveness. It may be something that takes time.

What things are not useful for you that you need to get rid of? They may not necessarily be bad things, but they cause clutter and are not helpful for you to carry. It could be something like worrying about a situation you can't control, or a habit that distracts you from the presence of God.

Just as you sort out your post when it comes through, clean your living space on a regular basis or take your car for its MOT, doing a spiritual clean out is something that is good to revisit at regular occasions with God. In different seasons He might show you different things.

Get a pen ready and sit down with God. Ask God to show you something that He wants you to hold on to in this season. How does He want you to take hold of this?

Ask Him to reveal to you one action that you need to take before you can move on. What is it that you need to do and when is the next opportunity that you can do it?

Ask Him to show you something that you need to let go of. Practically, what does it look like for you to let go of this? If it is not something that is material, it might be good to do a prophetic act of letting go of it.

It's good to ask God about each of these things as they may not be things you are immediately aware of. Have a chat about each of them with God.

God's Masterpiece

'For we are His workmanship, created in Christ Jesus unto good works, which God hath before ordained that we should walk in them.'

Ephesians 2:10 (KJV)

n Genesis 1, God speaks into being the land, the oceans, the plants and animals, the sun, moon and stars and everything that exists. *'God saw that it was good.' (Genesis 1:25)*

Then God creates mankind. *'God saw all that He had made, and it was very good.' (Genesis 1:31)* Not just good, but very good!

Ephesians 2:10, says *'For we are His workmanship.'*

The Greek word for 'workmanship' that Paul uses is 'poiema', which in different versions is translated as *'handiwork'* (NIV), *'masterpiece'* (NLT), and *'His own master work, a work of art'* (AMP).

It's also the root from which we get the English word poetry. We are God's expertly crafted poetry, where each word and detail is intentionally chosen and carefully selected!

Each of us individually are God's masterpieces because we are all handmade by Him. But collectively, we as humans are God's masterpiece. We all look, sound and act differently from each other and we have different giftings and talents. We have different *'good works'* and pathways that God has prepared for us in advance.

That is where our collective beauty lies: in our uniqueness and in our individuality.

It's important that we see both ourselves and others through the lens of how God sees us. When we see people from our heavenly Father's perspective, we see them with love, compassion and joy. We see them as image bearers of God, all reflecting the beauty of our Maker.

Just as an artist signs their name on their canvas, we carry God's signature and His fingerprints because we are made by Him and created in His image. We are like signposts pointing towards His glory and goodness.

So *'Arise, shine, for your light has come, and the glory of the Lord rises upon you'! (Isaiah 60:1)*

☙ RESPONSE

Ask God to show you a picture of what it looked like when He made you. What is the look on His face as He is carefully crafting you? What qualities and characteristics is He bringing together? What does He rejoice in as He is making you?

The next time you are tempted to judge someone or are frustrated with someone, take a second to change your spiritual glasses and ask God to show you how He sees them. Why not ask God for a picture of what it looked like when He was carefully crafting that person? What does God rejoice in about that person?

The Extraordinary Ordinary

'Listen and hear My voice; pay attention and hear what I say.'

Isaiah 28:23

It might be easy to praise God and give thanks in the great moments. It might be natural to turn to God in the difficult moments. But what about all the in-between moments?

When I'm having a pretty good day, everything is going to plan and I have nothing to complain about, I can sometimes forget my need for God. When it's just another day doing the same routine, I can so easily forget to give thanks.

I am learning that God is just as present in the small, everyday moments as He is in the dramatic highs and lows. Well, I guess I believed that, but I didn't really expect to encounter Him in all the small moments.

I didn't expect God to have anything in particular to say to me while I was eating my breakfast. I didn't expect Him to reveal His thoughts about me through a strange dream I had. I didn't expect Him to speak to me through a random song I had stuck in my head. I didn't expect Him to make me laugh as I fall asleep at night. Yet He does all those things!

In Psalm 16:8 David says, *'I have set the Lord always before me.' (KJV)*

David intentionally fixes his eyes on God every day. He praised God in the victories and ran to God in times of despair, but he also modelled a life of intentional, daily communion in all the in-between times too.

The thing is, when you invite God into your ordinary moments, He actually makes them rather extraordinary! I'm not necessarily talking about big miracles or dramatic encounters, but how extraordinary to discover the thoughts of God? How extraordinary to speak one to one with the Holy Spirit?

In these every day, in-between moments, God is not silent: we just need to listen. He is not on standby: we need to take ourselves off spiritual standby! If I linger long enough to explore that passing spontaneous thought, I might just learn something new about my Maker.

Let's *expect* that God will show up in our everyday moments. I pray these small, extraordinary moments will become my new ordinary!

Is there something you could do that would remind you of God's presence with you throughout the day? Be creative with it!

I know some people who attach a buzzer to their clothing that vibrates at regular intervals throughout the day. Only they notice it, but it prompts them to tune into God's presence. I once walked around for a year with a stone in my shoe to remind me of God with me wherever I walked! (Although I maybe wouldn't recommend that one!) Could you put a picture or Bible verse somewhere in your house where you would regularly see it and be reminded of His presence with you? Could you set some kind of alarm to go off at regular intervals throughout the day?

Uncomfortable Waiting...

'Be still before the Lord and wait patiently for Him.'

Psalm 37:7

For the Queen's Platinum Jubilee in June 2022, I thought it would be a good opportunity to get to know my neighbours more by planning a small street party.

On the day, I started taking tables, chairs, cakes, mugs and decorations outside. Eventually when everything was set up, I made myself a coffee, sat down, and waited...

Not many people walk past my street, but I still started to become very aware that I looked a bit silly sitting there by myself with a big table of cakes and a lot of empty chairs!

A man walking his dog on the neighbouring street looked at me and said, 'Party for one?' I laughed awkwardly and quickly said something to assure him that more people were coming!

After a very long ten minutes, I heard a door open and people from across the street came out to join me! It wasn't long before more people came out with their families and pets and soon, we had a nice little gathering! It was a lovely time of getting to know each other and enjoying being out on the street where we all live.

After a couple of hours, people started to drift off to go about their days. I found myself sitting alone again with the empty chairs and a table half full of cakes. There was still some time left, but I really wanted to pack up and go in. It was getting cold and surely no one else was going to come now!

But just as I was about to go in, one more person came! We ended up having a lovely chat, and she even helped me clear everything away at the end.

It made me think: how willing am I to wait a bit longer, even when it is uncomfortable or awkward? I almost missed the last person who came, just because I didn't want to look foolish sitting there by myself!

How willing am I to wait a bit longer to see what God has got in store?

It might be a bit uncomfortable, but surely worth it in the end. I don't want to miss what God wants to do!

✒ RESPONSE

Next time you are spending some time in prayer or worship and are about to finish and move on, stay and wait a little bit longer. It's not something you need to be legalistic about every time, but just choosing occasionally to linger a bit longer often brings beautiful times of intimacy with God.

You don't need to feel anything in particular or hear anything, but just linger and rest in His presence. Even if it feels uncomfortable, just wait on the Lord a little bit longer. Enjoy that precious time with Him.

Knowing God

'If You are pleased with me, teach me Your ways so I may know You and continue to find favour with You.'

Exodus 33:13

Moses was hungry to know more of God. His desire was to understand God's ways so that he could know God more intimately and walk in step with His plans.

I know many who have a hunger and thirst to really know God more: not just to know about Him, but to have an experiential knowledge of His love where we have an immovable understanding of who He is at the very core of our being.

This happens in the secret place, when we spend time being with God and learning what He sounds like, what He thinks and what He is doing.

I think it also happens as we seek to be more aware of Him in our everyday lives. If we want to really know God, we need to do life with Him, and not just meet Him at set "appointments".

Paul prayed that the church in Ephesus may know God better:

> *'I keep asking that the God of our Lord Jesus Christ, the glorious Father, may give you the Spirit of wisdom and revelation, so that you may know Him better.' (Ephesians 1:17)*

We can grow in our knowledge of God through the Spirit of wisdom and revelation, which is good news for us because it means we don't have to strive to know God. It is through grace that we can get to know Him more, guided by the Spirit as He reveals truths to us about who He is.

When God does a new thing, it will always be in line with His character and His word. So, let's seek to really know God through spending time with Him and through reading the Bible so that we will be able to recognise and discern where God is moving, not necessarily because we've seen it before, but because it is in alignment with who He is.

Surely knowing and loving God and being known and loved by Him is the greatest joy we can have!

⟩ RESPONSE

Sit down with God and ask Him to show you something new about Him or a different side to His character. You might want to pick a name of God in the Bible and ask Him to show you what this looks like.

For example, Healer, Provider, Strong Tower, Prince of Peace, Shepherd, Ancient of Days etc.

For instance, you could say, "Lord, will you show me how you are my Banner?" (*Jehovah Nissi – Exodus 17:15*) You might get a picture, a phrase, an impression or a sense of revelation. Write/draw what you see/hear.

What About the Rest?

> 'Then, because so many people were coming and
> going that they did not even have a chance to eat,
> He said to them, "Come with Me by yourselves to
> a quiet place and get some rest."'
>
> Mark 6:31

I think resting well is pretty hard. Especially in our culture of hustle and striving, it seems counterintuitive to spend time not being "productive". It takes a lot of trust to rest, especially when there are always things we could be doing.

Jesus invites us to live from a place of rest. He modelled this in His ministry. Rest wasn't something He did at the end of a long week when all the work was done. He didn't push Himself to a place where His only option was to collapse in a heap in order to recover enough to keep going a bit longer.

In Jesus' ministry, there were always people to heal and crowds to teach. But in the middle of all this, He prioritised spending time with God frequently. He lingered in prayer. He meditated on Scripture. He spent time just sitting in God's presence, not doing anything "productive". He purposefully and intentionally withdrew from the hustle and bustle.

He also worked from a place of rest. He was never striving and never hurried around. He constantly carried peace and stillness because in everything, He rested in His Father and was guided by the Spirit.

Can we trust God enough with our time to prioritise rest with Him in the middle of our work, not just at the end when everything is done?

Resting well is abiding in God, not in our worries or our to-do list. I think it takes practice and perseverance to be able to rest well. Rest was a priority for Jesus, and it is also a gift from God to us.

So how can we take a small step in the coming days towards making rest more of a priority rather than a last resort when all the work is done? What does it look like to work from a place of peace and rest?

Ask God to reveal to you any moments or occasions in your everyday life where you are not working or moving from a place of rest. Ask Him how you can take a step towards resting in Him in your everyday life. Does it mean taking a moment to fix your eyes on Jesus before stepping into a situation? Does it mean not looking at your phone at a certain time of day? Does it mean developing a new rhythm of prayer?

Write down when you feel restful. Write down things you enjoy doing that bring you joy and delight and peace. Is there a step you can take towards intentionally making more time for these things?

Do you ever feel guilty for resting? If so, ask God to reveal to you where you first picked this up. Ask Him what He wants to tell you about rest that you can lean on in place of what you have been believing. Write this down so you can go back to it if you ever feel that you shouldn't rest because of guilt or pressure.

Stepping Stones

'The Lord is compassionate and gracious, slow
to anger, abounding in love.'

Psalm 103:8

I went for a walk one day by a stream which had some stepping stones. It looked easy at first, but then as I started going
along, some were a bit trickier than others and some began
to wobble.

Thankfully, I made it to the other side without touching
the water, but there were moments when I wasn't sure if I would
make it or not!

However, the stream wasn't very deep and I could see the
bottom the whole time. I knew that if I did fall off, I might have
to deal with squelching socks, but it wouldn't be disastrous.
Plus, I would know that where I stepped last time was a bit slippery, so I could try again and alter my balance or try stepping
somewhere else.

I think this is a good picture of what it looks like as we walk through life with God.

Because we're on stepping stones, it does often mean there is a bit of risk in taking the next step. But because they are stepping stones, the water can't be too deep.

As I was going along, I needed to concentrate on the stepping stone that was right in front of me. There was no point thinking about the tricky one coming up next because I might have lost my balance on the one I was on.

I was keeping in mind where I was heading – the bank on the other side - but I needed to keep my focus on what was right in front of me.

If we slip on a stone, even repeatedly, every time Jesus is there to give us a hand to step back up out of the water.

As the verse at the beginning says, the Lord is compassionate, gracious, slow to anger and abounding in love.

We might need to take some time to deal with our wet socks or revaluate where we step, but the loving Jesus is always with us on our journey, cheering us on!

Take some time to imagine stepping stones in front of you. Ask God to show you what these stepping stones look like for you in this season of your life.

Is it time to move across the stones quickly, or is it time to rest on the stone you are on? Can you see where you are heading? Are there any slippery stones He is highlighting where you might need to be careful? Let Jesus take you through the scene and show you what you need to see.

From the verse at the beginning, take each of the words and phrases: 'compassionate', 'gracious', 'slow to anger' and 'abounding in love'. Say each of these out loud and meditate on them. What does it mean for God to be each of these things? Take some time to gain deeper understanding of these aspects of God's character.

No Words

'As she stood there behind Him at His feet weep-
ing, she began to wet His feet with her tears. Then
she wiped them with her hair, kissed them and
poured perfume on them.'

Luke 7:38

While Jesus was having dinner at the house of
Simon the Pharisee, a woman came, uninvited,
and poured out a whole jar of very expensive
perfume on Jesus. She gave everything to Him, pouring out her
financial security and facing judgement from those around her.

She doesn't say anything to Jesus, but she speaks of love,
adoration, worship and thanks all in a single act. There were
no words in that moment that could sum up her gratitude and
love for Jesus.

As Jesus stood before the Sanhedrin after His arrest, the chief priests shouted false accusations against him, *'But Jesus remained silent and gave no answer.' (Mark 14:61)*

I'm sure Jesus didn't have a lack of words, but instead He chose to let His life speak. His death and resurrection speak of His awesome power and unquantifiable love poured out for us.

I find myself with a lack of words to describe how I feel when I think of what Jesus went through on my behalf.

Like Barabbas, we all have a cross with our name on. Then Jesus steps in, completely innocent and undeserving of the cross, and *takes our place.* He suffers more than any of us could imagine, because He loves us.

No words.

Like the woman who anointed Jesus, when you have no words, let your actions speak instead. Pour out everything to him, expecting nothing in return, just because He is worthy of your everything.

Pour out your heart in worship.

Pour out your soul in thanks.

Pour out love to everyone around you.

Because Jesus poured out *everything* for us.

Read the story of Jesus taking Barabbas' place on the cross in Matthew 27:15-26. Now imagine yourself in the story in the place of Barabbas. See Jesus standing next to you, completely innocent. How do you feel as the crowds are shouting? What is the look on Jesus' face?

Imagine the moment where Pilate washes his hands, signifying that Jesus will be crucified in place of you. Is there anything you want to say to Jesus? Is there anything you want to do? How do you feel as Jesus is taken away to be crucified and you are set free?

The Power of Testimony

'For the testimony of Jesus is the spirit of prophecy.'

Revelation 19:10 KJV

When we share testimonies of what God has done, it opens up an avenue of faith for us to say, "Do it again God!" Testimonies raise our faith and fix our focus on the God of miracles.

I believe there is real power when it comes to speaking out what God has done. Here is my testimony about testimony:

I once had some pain in my left knee which had really been bothering me in the night. Whilst at a teaching session about healing, I asked a couple of people to pray for my knee and they did. As I tested it out, I felt that it was a tiny bit better.

The leaders then asked if anyone had any improvement and would like to come and share a testimony. I wasn't very keen because I wasn't completely sure if it was actually better or not, but no one else was going so I went up.

I very briefly shared how I had received prayer and my knee felt a tiny bit better, then scuttled back to my seat. But as I was going back, I instantly felt God heal my knee completely! I felt the pain disappear and felt an impact in my spirit, so I knew without a doubt that I was healed. Even though I had been reluctant to share a testimony, it was like the speaking out of what God had done had released the full healing!

The pain did come back later on, however I absolutely knew that I had been healed in that moment, so in the coming days I kept thanking God for my healing. A few days later I had absolutely no pain at all. I still have no lingering symptoms. My knee is completely well to this day!

So, let's celebrate the Lord and what He has done by sharing testimonies with each other!

Even if it seems small or insignificant, don't disqualify yourself because there is great power in speaking out your testimony. It's something that God has done for you that you can't deny, and nobody can take that away from you.

RESPONSE

Can you think of a story you have that testifies to the goodness of God? Write it down if you haven't already. Writing it out helps to clarify it in your mind so it is easier to share. It could a story of when you first accepted Jesus. It could be a story of healing, breakthrough, provision, family reconciliation or answered prayer.

Is there an opportunity for you to share this story with others to encourage them, maybe in church or in a small group? Are there any friends or family members that you could share it with? Could you share it with someone who doesn't yet know Jesus? Plan a time when you can share this story.

The Creative Gene

"So God created mankind in His own image, in the image of God He created them; male and female He created them."

Genesis 1:27

God is the ultimate Creator. All we have to do is look around to see the vastness and diversity of His creation. It is endless and full of beauty, richness, patterns, colours and nuances. God never gets tired of being creative!

Yet, what we currently see is only a foretaste of what we will experience in heaven! I can't wait to see all the goodness and beauty that God has in store for us.

When we consider God's vastness and splendour, it's incredible to think that we are His image bearers. We are all creators too in different ways; we've inherited that creative gene from our Father.

When I think of creativity, the first things that often spring to mind are the typical "creative arts" like painting, drawing, dancing, music, etc. These things seem to be the most socially recognised forms of creativity. However, it is so much wider than that. Creativity includes things like cooking, problem solving, innovating, writing, speaking, pioneering, photography, communicating, teaching etc. and there are so many more!

Creativity is the ability to imagine, envisage and dream up a new idea or concept and to bring that something into existence. We all have that ability. We might have strengths in different areas and some people may seem more creative than others, but creativity is at the centre of how we were made.

When children play, their creativity is endless! As we grow up, many of us lose touch with our creative, childlike nature because of fear, inhibitions, apathy or general lack of use as we go about our daily adult lives. We seem to have lost our dreaming capacity.

However, it doesn't mean we've lost our ability to be creative! We might just need to exercise that creative muscle.

God loves it when we work in partnership with Him in our creativity! Our creativity can help us to discover more about God the Creator and who He has created us to be. Creativity is powerful and indispensable.

RESPONSE

Sit with God and write down your creative gifts. Is there something that you love to do that involves creativity? Is there something that you are good at that involves envisioning something new? When was the last time you exercised these gifts? If it's not something you normally do, can you set aside some time for that activity?

Why not try something completely new? If you don't normally paint, for example, why not give it a go? Have you ever tried writing poetry? Delight in the process of trying something new with God, without any expectations of an end result.

Take some time to delight in nature today. Stop and notice the intricacies of God's creation. What do you learn about God as you look at what He has created?

Extravagant Praise

'Let them praise His name with dancing.'

Psalm 149:3

God is not static. He is a moving God.

In Genesis 1:2, *'the Spirit of God moved upon the face of the waters.' (KJV)* The Hebrew word for *'moved'* also means fluttering and shaking.

In Zephaniah 3:17, it says God *'will rejoice over you with singing'* where the Hebrew meaning is to spin around under a violent emotion of joy!

God even claps His hands when He says, *'I too will strike My hands together and My wrath will subside.' (Ezekiel 21:17)*

Not only is it natural for God to move, but it's also a natural response for us to praise God with dancing, stamping, clapping, jumping, lifting our hands, bowing down etc.

We see many examples of physical praise in the Bible, for example, when Miriam picked up her tambourine and led the women in a dance of praise in Exodus 15:20, or when David danced with all his might before the ark of the Lord in 2 Samuel 6:14.

In Nehemiah 8:6, *'all the people lifted their hands and responded, "Amen! Amen!" Then they bowed down and worshiped the Lord with their faces to the ground.'*

Maybe you have an urge to lift up your hands or jump up and down or bow low to the ground whilst praising God. Don't ignore it! Movement is not foreign to God and it's not something we invented. It's our natural response to the glory of God! He created our physical bodies to move, so let's use them to give Him our highest and most extravagant praise.

Don't let the fear of man be a block to stop you from physically moving in response to God. It's powerful when there is the freedom to move and dance in corporate worship and I believe we need more of this, but we must keep this extravagant worship rooted in the secret place where only God can see. Don't feel you have to start by leaping up to the front of church in a wild dance with 10 flags! The best place to start is just by moving in your own home when no one else is around.

Never forget your audience of three: Father, Jesus and Holy Spirit!

🐦 RESPONSE

Set aside some time for worship today, preferably alone where no one can see so you won't be distracted or self-conscious. Put on some of your favourite worship music. Does it make you want to move? What is your initial physical response to the presence of God? Have you ever danced in worship before? Try it out!

Some more ideas: you could imagine the Holy Spirit all around you, surrounding you like water. What does it look like to move in Him? Ask Jesus to show you what it looks like when He dances and copy His movements. Ask God to show you what movements the angels are doing in worship and see if you can copy their movements too! Are there particular movements that you feel you want to do in response to God?

Getting Your Feet Wet

'Now the Jordan is at flood stage all during harvest. Yet as soon as the priests who carried the ark reached the Jordan and their feet touched the water's edge, the water from upstream stopped flowing.'

Joshua 3:15-16

When I think of this story of the Israelites crossing the Jordan River into the promised land, I have always imagined the river as a narrow trickling stream. But the Jordan River is on average between 3 - 10 feet deep and 90 -100 feet wide. As it was the harvest and the river was at flood stage, we can assume the river was more than 10 feet deep and more than 100 feet wide when the Israelites crossed! Now imagine being one of those Levitical priests standing at the edge of the river whilst carrying the weighty, precious ark of God ... and Joshua says to step right in!

The priests had to actually get their feet wet before the water was cut off. It would have been easy to see the river dry up before their eyes and then step out, but they were asked to take that step of faith before they actually saw God move.

That's why it's called a step of faith, because there is an element of risk in stepping out. This story is so relevant to our everyday lives. We might see an opportunity to pray for someone, but we will only see God step in when we actually step out and pray! Or maybe you feel a prompting to give financially when humanly speaking, you can't really afford it. How much can we actually take God at His word that He is our provider and take that step of faith?

God is on our side. He's got our backs. Unless we're deliberately going against Him, when we step out, He'll show up.

> 'The Lord Himself goes before you and will be
> with you; He will never leave you nor forsake
> you. Do not be afraid; do not be discouraged.'
> (Deuteronomy 31:8)

Even if it feels like we are stepping out alone, the Lord actually goes before us. We can be confident that when we step out, God will be with us and cover us because we are His children and He loves us.

Do you believe that God will step in when you step out? Are you willing to take a risk? If God is who He says He is, how risky is it really?

Is there a situation where you feel God is asking you to step out, but it requires faith and a bit of risk? Take this situation to God. Ask Him if there are specific steps to take.

Envision what it looks like for you to step out in this situation. Where is God as you take that step of faith? What does He want you to know as you step out? What is He speaking over you?

Write down some promises of God that you can lean on for faith. Write down where He has been faithful and trustworthy in your life so far. Write down where you have seen evidence of Him being faithful in other people's lives. It's good to remind yourself of these things regularly.

Rejoice Always

'The joy of the Lord is your strength.'

Nehemiah 8:10

B ecause of Jesus, we can find joy every day. After all, the Bible says, *'in Thy presence is fulness of joy' (Psalm 16:11 KJV).*

I love that word fullness. It gives me a picture of God just bursting with good things and overflowing with joy!

There is a wonderful kind of joy that can be found in doing good for others, when you sacrificially give time or resources without expecting anything in return. There's a joy in stopping and taking time just for one person. In God's kingdom there is overflowing abundance, so as sons and daughters we can give out of that abundance.

There's a unique kind of joy to be found in having secrets with God. I don't mean secret sin, but things like giving in secret or having a song that you sing only for him. Sometimes there are little jewels He reveals to us that are just for us, and there is joy in treasuring those in your heart.

Sometimes if I try to be too "grown up" it takes the joy out of things. I think part of growing in maturity in the kingdom is actually learning to become more childlike in our relationship with God. That's why I love to dance because it stops me taking myself too seriously! I like finding the joy in being childlike as an adult.

It can be trickier to find joy in difficult times, but I believe that with Jesus with us, we can always experience His joy. I don't mean just putting on a brave face or neglecting trials, but I think there is joy to be found when you have to lean more fully on God. Joy in difficult times doesn't really make sense to the world, but it can only make sense because Jesus is present and never changing. It's a kind of joy that's rooted in an eternal perspective.

> 'Now is your time of grief, but I will see you again and you will rejoice, and no one will take away your joy.' (John 16:22)

Jesus says that post-resurrection, no one will take away our joy. Jesus' resurrection is sure and complete, so our joy can also be sure because of our certainty in eternity!

RESPONSE

At the end of your day, take a moment to look back through the events of the day. Where were the moments of joy? Were there specific moments that made you smile? Take some time to thank God for these moments.

If there were difficult times in your day, look back at them now with God. What does He have to say about them? Ask Him to show you where He was in these moments and find joy in knowing He was with you. Is there anything else He wants you to know about these moments? You could journal and write down how you felt to help you process them.

Zoom Out

'He is before all things, and in Him all things hold together. And He is the head of the body, the church; He is the beginning and the firstborn from among the dead, so that in everything He might have the supremacy.'

Colossians 1:17-18

D o you ever wake up really happy one day and the next day a bit tired and grumpy for no apparent reason? It can be so easy to get caught up with the small irritants of life. Things are always changing around us whether it be our emotions, our circumstances, the weather, the food prices etc.

The thing is, even if I'm having a bad day, God is not! If I'm feeling down, it doesn't mean God is any less powerful. If I'm feeling tired, it doesn't change the fact that Jesus is still working and moving.

Sometimes I think it's helpful to take a moment to zoom out. Zoom out of your own bubble so you can see the awesomeness and greatness and majesty of Jesus. Zoom out and see how God is holding the whole world in the palm of His hand. Zoom out and see time from God's perspective, where *a thousand years in Your sight are like a day that has just gone by.' (Psalm 90:4)*

Let's take refuge in the big picture. The big picture is that Jesus has won! He is victorious and undefeated. He is building His church and His kingdom is coming. Let's meditate on those famous words of Jesus on the cross: *'It is finished.' (John 19:30)* He has overcome the world!

Meditating on the big picture with Jesus at the centre gives us a security that cannot be shaken, no matter what is changing around us.

Some people say that the only constant in this world is change. Yet, through all change, God remains constant.

Take some time to zoom out and rest in the greatness and security of who God is. In Him, all things hold together.

> *'The heavens are Yours, and Yours also the earth; You founded the world and all that is in it.' (Psalm 89:11)*

Or as the song goes, "He's got the whole world in His hands!"

RESPONSE

Take some time today to meditate on the greatness and vastness of God. Julian of Norwich[1] describes how as she considered a small hazelnut in her hand, she received revelation about how God made everything that exists, how He loves His creation and how He sustains it all.

Take a small spherical object in your hand – it could be a hazelnut or something like a marble or a grape. Reflect on how God is holding the whole world in the palm of His hand. Meditate on how God sustains everything. Meditate on His unquantifiable love for His creation.

Re-read the verse at the beginning and reflect on the glorious supremacy of Jesus and how through Him, all things hold together.

[1] Julian of Norwich (c. 1342 – c. 1416) was an anchorite. She wrote 'Revelations of Divine Love' based on 16 vision she received whilst seriously ill in 1373.